Quaker renewal

Craig Barnett

A *Friend* Publication

Published by:

The Friend Publications Limited

173 Euston Road, London NW1 2BJ

Charity registration number: 211649

Cover copyright: Pop Nukoonrat (ipopba) / 123RF Stock Photo

Printed and bound by:

Henry Ling Limited, The Dorset Press, Dorchester DT1 1HD

Set in Baskerville type

ISBN: 978-0-9954757-2-4

Printed on 100% recycled paper manufactured

from responsible and renewable sources

Contents

Other pieces

Preface

Craig Barnett is one of the most articulate voices in modern Quakerism and in recent years has engaged, directly and honestly, with many of the vital challenges facing the Religious Society of Friends.

His faith is rooted in his personal experience and his belief in the profound and transforming presence of the spiritual in every life. He writes: 'The religious path is not a self-improvement project. We do not need to labour to perfect ourselves, only to return to ourselves, to our capacity to listen and respond to the Inward Guide.'

This book is made up of a series of articles entitled 'Quaker renewal' that were commissioned for *the Friend* magazine. A selection of other pieces, written in recent years, is also included. In these essays Craig offers a deeply felt, perceptive and clear analysis of contemporary Quakerism and considers the way forward. At the heart of this book is a fundamental question: What does it mean to be a Quaker?

Thanks are due to the trustees of The Friend Publications Limited, particularly Geoffrey Durham, and to all those involved in the production of this book, especially Elinor Smallman, production and office manager of *the Friend*.

Ian Kirk-Smith

Editor, the Friend

About the author

Craig Barnett lives with his family in Sheffield, where he works for a local refugee charity. He was one of the founders of the national City of Sanctuary movement and has also worked as director of the Hlekweni Friends Training Centre in Zimbabwe.

He writes regular short essays on Quaker themes at: *transitionquaker.blogspot.co.uk*

Introduction

Renewal of the Society waits for the choice of each Friend: Am I willing to risk the disturbing, transfiguring presence of the Spirit in my life? To obey it? To expect 'the Cross' and dark days as I discover and nurture who I am before God? When we choose to live the spiritual life the Quaker Way, these are the experiences we are committing ourselves to, whatever words we put upon them. If significant numbers of us are not interested in, or willing to live by these experiences, the hoped-for renewal of our meetings cannot occur. But if our collective spiritual power gathers strength it will infect other Friends and newcomers. Ministry will become more grounded in the Spirit and individuals will be inspired by the Spirit to serve our meetings as nurturers, prophets and conservers.

Ursula Jane O'Shea
Living the Way: Quaker spirituality and community

There are good reasons why long-lived religious movements need to be continually renewed. As formal structures and bureaucracies develop, members' energy is increasingly drawn into perpetuating the organisation, rather than serving the original spiritual mission of the community.

The organisation's culture and structures soon become closely geared to the interests of its most influential members. These structures eventually push increasing numbers of spiritually seeking members to the edges of the community, or even out of it altogether.

This is very much the situation I see in large parts of Britain Yearly Meeting. As a Friend in one struggling Meeting asked recently after a talk on 'vibrant Meetings': 'We already have too much to do. Are we supposed to be vibrant now as well?'

We currently have an organisational culture and structures that suit a dwindling group of members in many scattered, mostly very tiny Meetings. A wider group of attenders come to Meeting semi-regularly to recharge their batteries on a Sunday morning, but are deterred from getting more involved by the onerous demands of administration or the absence of real spiritual vitality.

Most of the newcomers who occasionally turn up to try a Quaker Meeting on Sunday never come back, or attend for only a short time before drifting off to look for something more spiritually nourishing. Yet we rarely ask ourselves what it is that might be missing from our worship and our community.

In large part, British Quakers are asleep; but we are stirring. A growing number of voices are asking whether the way we have come to 'do Quakerism' over the last few decades really serves the needs of our communities or the leadings of the Spirit. Many Meetings have confronted their settled opposition to 'proselytising', and started to actively encourage new attenders to our Meetings. Some Friends are even starting to question the hardened liberal dogmas that have outlawed the teaching of Quaker spirituality and the ministry of leadership in our communities.

These fitful stirrings have not yet reached a critical threshold of awakening. We may be at a crucial point in our story as British Quakers. Will we toss and turn, only to roll over and go back to sleep? Or will we come awake at last, while we still have enough energy and hope to renew our Society and ourselves, to realise the unique possibilities of a renewed Quaker way for our times?

We have been here before. At the very end of the nineteenth century the 'Quaker Renaissance' movement introduced the era of liberal Quakerism. This renewed form of the Quaker way unleashed a new wave of spiritual vigour and social engagement.

to the heroic achievements of Friends during the twentieth century, from conscientious objection to the Kindertransport, humanitarian relief and anti-war movements. We need a new kind of 'Quaker Renaissance' today that takes seriously the potential of the Quaker way to connect us with the source of life and power that can renew our lives, build up loving communities and heal the wounds of the world.

The short essays in this collection are attempts to point towards some areas where I see potential for new life and creativity in Quaker spirituality and practice. Essential to realising these possibilities is a willingness to share our questions, insights and frustrations with each other, without evading the risks of mutual challenge and vulnerability. This is not easy; it can create discomfort and conflict, but we cannot be a religious community without it.

These essays necessarily include judgements about our current Quaker culture that will not be shared by other Friends whose experience and temperament are very different to mine. This is just as it should be. I don't want to argue that my suggestions should be accepted by everyone. If they stimulate some reflection and conversation about the possibilities of a more life-giving Quaker way for our time, they will have served their purpose.

Craig Barnett

Quaker renewal

Quaker renewal

Quaker renewal

The Quaker way

Over recent years many Friends have diagnosed a crisis in Britain Yearly Meeting. They have warned us of a continuing decline in membership, and of intractable conflicts over religious belief and language. These concerns are important, but I believe that both are actually symptoms of a more fundamental crisis of spiritual vitality.

Throughout our history Quakers have faced the challenge of continually renewing our spiritual life and shared practice. Every generation has had to rediscover the Quaker way anew. We all need to confront our own spiritual inertia and find the depth of reality in our own experience. Since most Quakers now join as older adults, we also have to learn the Quaker way as a 'second language'. This requires us to avoid projecting onto the Quaker community the assumptions, hurts or disappointments we have received from other traditions.

These challenges have become especially acute in recent years. For several decades we have neglected to explicitly teach core Quaker practices to newcomers, with the result that many Meetings have little experience of gathered worship, Spirit-led discernment or lives rooted in responsiveness to divine leadings. These are the substance of the Quaker path. Without them we are too often left with the forms of 'Quakerliness' without the experiential substance, and inevitably we fall into disputes over words.

In the absence of any shared understanding of core Quaker practices such as Meetings for Worship and for Business, we increasingly encounter chronic disagreements about how to live the Quaker way together. A shared understanding does not mean identical beliefs, but it does rely on a common language for communicating our experiences, explicit teaching and learning, and a continual conversation about the meaning and purpose of our core practices. In the absence of these a Quaker Meeting can become simply a neutral space for the sharing of ideas from other religious traditions or secular ideologies.

Thankfully, there are signs of awakening. A growing number of voices are asking whether the way we have come to 'do Quakerism' over the last few decades really serves the needs of our communities or the leadings of the Spirit. Some Meetings are experimenting with new or rediscovered forms of outreach, worship and teaching. They are encouraging the sharing of spiritual experience, instead of evading the risks of encounter, by focusing solely on the safer topics of shared political and ethical values.

What this highlights to me is that the rediscovery of our Quaker tradition as a living way of spiritual practice is in our own hands. If we want a deeper experience of community, and a renewed spiritual depth of worship and testimony, we need to take courage. We have to create opportunities for conversations about the meaning of our Quaker practices with each other and throughout the Religious Society of Friends.

We can encourage each other to take the Quaker way seriously as a path of spiritual practice to learn about, to discuss with each other, and above all to work at, allowing it to change us and the world around us.

Centre and boundary

Most of us are understandably wary of drawing boundaries around what counts as being a Quaker, as any boundary risks excluding someone. Yet the absence of any shared understanding of the Quaker way is experienced as an obstacle to communication and to community in many of our Meetings. It becomes ever harder to explain to newcomers what the Quaker Meeting is for, and to resolve our own practical disagreements, as our concern to include everyone makes it increasingly difficult to find a common basis for Quaker identity.

Some Friends have tried to define the boundaries of Quaker identity by identifying certain core Quaker beliefs, such as 'that of God in everyone'. Others point to a list of testimonies, which are often interpreted as 'shared values' rather than Spirit-led actions. For some, there is no specific teaching or content to the Quaker way at all. For these Friends, the Quaker Meeting is simply an accepting space for people to explore their own values and pursue their own private spiritual journeys.

I believe that a more fruitful way to look at what it means to be a Quaker is to focus not on the 'boundary' but on the 'centre' of the Quaker way. For me, the centre of our tradition is not beliefs or values, but a small number of distinctive Quaker practices for worship, discernment and testimony. Foremost among these are the Meeting for Worship and the Meeting for Worship for Business.

Quaker practices have never been static. Meetings for Worship have changed a great deal since the seventeenth century, when they could last for three hours and contain lengthy Biblical sermons.

New practices also emerge over time – including worship sharing, Meetings for Clearness and Experiment with Light – and they are always subject to adaptation and reinterpretation. But it is through our participation in these practices, including in discussions about their meaning, that we take part in the Quaker way.

All of our Quaker practices are grounded in spiritual discernment. They require us to develop the capacity for attentive listening to divine leadings and to restrain our natural impulses towards self-assertion and defensiveness. Discernment is a form of perception – a practice of insight into a depth of reality that we can trust to guide us, as individuals and as communities.

All of our practices rely on a shared trust that there is a reliable source of guidance to be found, which is not simply a projection of our own wishes and values. This inner attitude of trust does not assume any particular theology; it is compatible with many kinds of religious belief and even with a thorough-going agnosticism. All that is essential is our practical willingness to listen for and to follow the leadings of the 'Inward Guide'.

The 'centre' of the Quaker way is to participate fully in the core Quaker practices that create the possibility of shared experiences and common understandings. This includes a commitment to continuing growth in appreciating the depths of possibility of these practices, in dialogue with other Friends throughout our Yearly Meeting and beyond.

If we focused on a commitment to Quaker practices as the centre of the Quaker way, perhaps we wouldn't need to worry so much about the boundaries. There is nothing exclusive about Quaker practices. Anyone can begin to explore them in an experimental spirit, starting right where we are. There are no preconditions, beyond the simple willingness to encounter a source of guidance beyond our conscious intentions, values and attitudes – allowing it to lead us into a wider, more generous and Spirit-filled life.

A shared language

One of the ways that contemporary Quaker practice has become impoverished is by the loss of a shared spiritual language. We have come to assume that the only way we can communicate at all is by trying to 'translate' each other's words into some other terms that are meaningful for us. This may work when our experiences are similar enough that we are 'just using different words to talk about the same thing'. But it doesn't help us to hear and to take seriously Friends whose experience is significantly different to our own. By translating their words into our own preferred language, we sidestep the reality of difference, instead of allowing ourselves to be challenged and enriched by it.

The absence of a shared language can also be an obstacle when we want to produce collective statements, such as minutes or outreach materials. If we try to include only words that no one will object to, we are left with an increasingly restricted vocabulary that is ever more dominated by the bureaucratic language of the wider culture.

There is an alternative. We could choose to cultivate a contemporary Quaker language that is rich enough to express the full diversity of our varied experiences. There is an extraordinarily creative spiritual vocabulary to draw upon in the writings of Quakers throughout our history. A contemporary language would also be continually open to whatever images, words and symbols arise from our current experience of Quaker practices.

A shared Quaker language would include multiple images and metaphors that reflect the multifaceted nature of spiritual reality.

Quaker practices open us to the possibility of encounter with a reality that may be experienced as personal and impersonal, masculine, feminine, immanent, transcendent or otherwise. So, words and symbols such as 'God', 'the Guide' or 'Inward Christ' might be recognised as valid ways of expressing the personal nature of some of our experiences – such as a sense of loving presence and guidance. At the same time, and without contradiction, such a language would also include impersonal images such as 'Light', 'Energy' or 'Oneness', which can point to experiences of illumination, empowerment and interrelationship.

A shared language would involve accepting all of these images as valid, but none of them as sufficient in themselves. It would be rich enough to enable everyone to express the depth and variety of our personal experiences. At the same time its diversity would point towards the inexpressible nature of spiritual reality, which is always beyond our capacity to fully name, identify or control. By acknowledging the validity of numerous ways of encountering spiritual reality, it would also create space for change and growth in our religious understanding, so we might be less inclined to rely on narrow theologically-defined identities.

Instead of defending our own concepts and images, and trying to exclude those used by other Friends, we might recognise a wide range of experiences, images and symbols as equally important for expressing the full range of Quaker experience.

Many of us also draw insight and inspiration from other religious traditions, and would continue to make use of other spiritual languages as well. But a sufficiently rich Quaker language would not depend on importing concepts from other traditions. It would be broad and subtle enough to communicate the breadth and depth of Quaker experience with each other and with the wider world – including the varied insights and commitments that arise from our shared Quaker practices and their practical expression in our lives.

Gathered worship

If the Quaker way has something unique to offer the world, perhaps it is the experience of a Gathered Meeting for Worship. This is what Gerald Hewitson has described as:

> ...a Meeting where the silence is as soft as velvet, as deep as a still pool; a silence where words emerge, only to deepen and enrich that rich silence, and where Presence is as palpable and soft as the skin of a peach; where the membrane separating this moment in time and eternity is filament-fine.

Journey into life, Swarthmore Lecture 2013

Gathered worship is the living power of the Quaker way, with an amazing capacity to heal, renew and transform our lives and communities. This depth of worship is a rare occurrence in some of our Meetings because the disciplines of listening and speaking that enable and sustain it are not being practised.

Worship is a movement of the whole being towards a spiritual reality that is ultimately mysterious. It requires the commitment of our whole selves – mind, heart, body and will – to something greater than our own values, thoughts and preferences. It is easy to keep ourselves at the centre, making worship into another activity of the conscious mind. The discipline of listening requires us to let go of our need to be in control. It asks us to open ourselves to a wordless encounter with the inward source of life and power – a sense of 'Presence' beyond thoughts and concepts. In that place we become receptive to the 'promptings of love and truth' that may arise to teach us, and that might require us to offer spoken ministry.

The discipline of speaking means discerning whether our intention to offer spoken ministry is a response to a specific leading of the Spirit. It asks us to relinquish the natural urge to speak from the needs of the ego. We have to learn to speak only when our message arises from the deeper place of responsiveness to spiritual reality.

When we minister from this place our simplest words have a special power to draw others into awareness, to encourage, to console or to challenge.

Where the disciplines of listening and speaking are not practised the Meeting for Worship can no longer function. Although the outward form may appear the same, such a Meeting has become something else. In these Meetings, spoken ministry tends toward political discussion or summaries of radio and television programmes. Friends tend to tolerate each other's messages in a spirit of generous forbearance, rather than embracing them as words with the power to speak to our hearts.

Elders have a particular responsibility for reminding Friends of the disciplines involved in Quaker worship. In practice, elders' willingness to do this is severely undermined by the insistence of many Friends that worship and ministry are purely subjective and not subject to community standards. For many years we have tried to avoid conflict within our Meetings by evading mutual accountability for the quality of our worship. We have not expected new Friends and attenders to learn the disciplines of Quaker worship. Instead, we have encouraged each other to reinterpret the practice of worship wherever it conflicts with our own preferences and assumptions.

Weekly Meeting for Worship cannot support the whole weight of our spiritual lives on its own. If our daily life is so hectic and overstretched that we come to Meeting with minds filled with jangling thoughts all clamouring for attention, we will miss the possibility of gathered worship. This is a struggle for many in a society that constantly pushes us into overwork, over-stimulation and over-consumption.

If we truly want to open ourselves to the possibilities of worship, we also need to make regular space in our daily lives for stillness and reflection, 'to set aside times of quiet for openness to the Holy Spirit... to find the inward source of our strength' (*Advices & queries* 3).

If a Quaker community is to exist as something beyond a social club for like-minded people, it needs to be rooted in an authentic experience of worship. A gathered Quaker Meeting has the power to heal, transform, embolden, to make us more sensitive and more aware. It is the life-giving sap that is needed for vital, outward-looking communities.

One of the greatest qualities of the Quaker way of worship is its utter simplicity. It needs no special building, no specially-qualified clergy or guru, no holy objects or texts. It is open to everyone on a basis of complete equality, without distinction of gender, sexuality or background. Quaker worship does not require special techniques or great natural ability, but it does demand our self-discipline and self-surrender:

> *Give over thine own willing, give over thy own running, give over thine own desiring to know or be anything and sink down to the seed which God sows in the heart, and let that grow in thee and be in thee and breathe in thee and act in thee; and thou shalt find by sweet experience that the Lord knows that and loves and owns that, and will lead it to the inheritance of Life, which is its portion.*

> Isaac Penington, 1661

Quaker renewal

The meaning of membership

Over recent decades membership has become a contested issue for British Quakers. Some Friends object to the membership process on principle, such as a supposed conflict with our testimony to equality, or are uneasy about the process of 'judging' who is acceptable to become a member.

It has become common for people to attend Meetings for many years without any intention of applying for membership. In many Meetings it is difficult to find Friends to fulfil all of the responsibilities that require membership, leading to the growing practice of appointing attenders to these roles. This appears to further undermine the meaningfulness of distinguishing between members and attenders at all.

Perhaps it is the way we have practised membership that has steadily eroded its meaning. *Quaker faith & practice* includes some quite clear statements about the core commitments involved in membership:

> *Membership is also a way of saying to the Meeting, and to the world, that you accept at least the fundamental elements of being a Quaker: the understanding of divine guidance, the manner of corporate worship and the ordering of the Meeting's business, the practical expression of inward convictions and the equality of all before God.* (11.01)

However, in many Area Meetings it is rare for these 'fundamental elements' to be mentioned at any point in the membership process. Instead, there often appears to be little or no standard for membership at all, beyond the individual's desire to join.

The consequence over many years is that being a member no longer means that someone shares a commitment to any specifically Quaker understandings, testimony or practices.

Renewal of our Society's spiritual roots in core Quaker practices calls for a reassessment of our membership process. For a religious society without a separate class of leaders, membership provides an opportunity for newcomers to make a deliberate act of commitment to the Quaker community and to assume a full share of responsibility for its governance. The membership process also offers a way to recognise and celebrate an inner transition from 'seeker' to 'convinced' Friend, and a commitment to upholding collective discernment, such as our corporate testimonies.

Our Meetings could renew the practice of membership by making use of the advice in *Quaker faith & practice* 11.08 to 'nurture and support individuals of all ages so that they can develop a sense of belonging and an understanding of our shared beliefs, testimonies and spiritual discipline'. *Quaker faith & practice* also makes reference to the possibility of 'special nurturing or supporting Friends' who could accompany potential new members, both before and after the formal membership process, to offer supportive listening and sharing of experience.

The practicalities of setting up a more meaningful and helpful process for potential new members are straightforward enough. More fundamentally, however, they rely on shared discernment by the existing members of an Area Meeting about what the core commitments of Quaker membership should be. In many Meetings this is the real stumbling block to any improvement in membership practices. The current tendency is often to evade potential conflict by avoiding discussion about the requirements of membership.

We need to have a deeper conversation than this, one that is not afraid to question current assumptions, if we want to revive the meaning of membership and enable it to contribute to the spiritual renewal of our communities.

The gift of leadership

It is often claimed that Quakers don't have leaders, but this is not quite true. In a Quaker Meeting leadership is shared among Friends holding many roles – including clerks, elders, overseers, nominations, children's and outreach committees, among others, and it is also practised more informally by those who minister to the community in many different ways. All of these Friends need to exercise the gift of leadership.

Leadership is a form of service to the community. It enables things to happen by taking responsibility for supporting, enabling and encouraging others, and it is essential for any group to function.

The tasks of leadership are not usually highly visible or dramatic. They include motivating, encouraging, thanking and welcoming, making sure that information is shared and clear arrangements are made, helping the group to stay on-topic and summing up the outcomes of discussions. It is also a function of leadership to remind the group of 'right ordering' (the Quaker community's agreed processes) and to discourage the most vocal individuals from dominating a group. Good leaders support and enable others' gifts and leadings (including others' potential for leadership) instead of suppressing everyone else's initiative.

The Quaker approach to church government, which early Friends called 'Gospel Order', is a way of recognising and distributing leadership, while keeping it accountable to the community as a whole. In a Quaker Meeting authority means being 'authorised' by the community to exercise accountable leadership.

But there are many Friends today who see every suggestion of leadership as authoritarianism. Many of us have experienced groups where authority has been abused or monopolised. Some who have been hurt by the misuse of authority in other contexts come to a Quaker Meeting expecting it to be a 'leaderless group' where 'everyone is equal'. The testimony to equality is sometimes mistaken for a belief that everyone is the same, instead of recognising the equal value of our very different gifts and experiences.

This suspicion of leadership has contributed to a Quaker culture that often serves to squash individual initiative, responsibility and enthusiasm. Those in leadership roles may be accused of being hierarchical when they try to fulfil the responsibilities given to them by the Meeting as a whole. This creates a strong temptation to be timid about exercising leadership, for fear of provoking Friends who don't accept the authority of elders or other appointed roles. Part of the challenge for those who hold leadership responsibilities is to be faithful to the authority entrusted to them by the Meeting, even at the risk of being criticised or resented. Sometimes this may mean challenging Friends who insist on getting their own way in opposition to the discernment of the whole community. This, too, as difficult and sometimes painful as it is, is an essential form of service – helping to prevent the community from being bullied by its most aggressive members.

In those periods when the Quaker movement has thrived, there have always been significant numbers of Friends who have practised leadership on behalf of the community. The revitalisation of our Quaker communities relies on encouraging the development and expression of the gift of leadership within our Meetings. Quaker communities, as with all other human groups, need people who are willing to take a share of leadership responsibilities, including the difficult and challenging ones, in order to thrive. Leaders are not a special kind of people with extraordinary abilities. The principal quality needed for leadership is simply a willingness to embrace some responsibility for the flourishing of the whole community.

The simplified Meeting

In too many Quaker Meetings spiritual vitality is being stifled by the excessive demands of church government. Struggling to meet the ever-growing requirements of administration can take up so much of Friends' time and energy that there is little left over to devote to the practice of the Quaker way itself.

Bureaucratic overload subverts the ministry of nominations to discern Friends' gifts and leadings, turning it into a weary necessity of 'filling jobs'. Committees and roles are readily set up but very rarely laid down, even where they are clearly no longer serving the life of the Spirit. But as long as we keep on devoting most of our energies to simply keeping the structures going, we only postpone the profound changes that are actually needed.

Instead of continually working harder just to keep going, the renewal of our Quaker practice asks us to refocus on what is essential – serving the leadings of the Spirit rather than the demands of property and administration.

Quaker organisation is not an end in itself. All of our structures, committees, roles and property exist for just one purpose – to help us to attend to the Inward Guide and to follow it. All other functions are secondary to these, and wherever administrative tasks interfere with Friends' capacity to practise the Quaker way, they need to be reduced, shared with other Meetings or eliminated altogether. Instead of allowing ourselves to become societies for the preservation of historic buildings, we need to recall our vocation as communities of faithful discernment and testimony to divine leadings.

The essential responsibilities of a Quaker Meeting are those that enable our core practices of worship, discernment and testimony. Our Meetings for Worship and for Business are essential for our formation as a community that is responsive to divine guidance. Friends' leadings need the discernment of the Meeting, so that they can be recognised and supported by the community and lived out as our testimony to the world. For these spiritual practices, we need the service of Friends who, between them, can offer the ministries of clerking and pastoral care that enable our Meetings to be rightly ordered. All other roles and responsibilities, including for legal and financial matters, are entirely secondary.

Perhaps we should support our nominations committees in resisting the pressure to treat Quaker roles as jobs that must be filled. Instead, we could encourage them to concentrate on recognising Friends' gifts and providing opportunities to exercise them. We might consider adopting a new discipline – of no longer expecting anyone to fulfil more than one significant Quaker responsibility at a time, reducing the number of roles to suit the Friends available. In this way each of us might be able to concentrate on undertaking one Quaker ministry wholeheartedly, instead of continuing to spread ourselves ever more thinly across too many tasks.

Perhaps we also need to discern the particular ministry of our Local or Area Meeting – what are we called to as a local community of Friends? Is it to build an inclusive and caring local community, to offer our testimony by challenging social injustices, to engage in interfaith learning and dialogue, or something else?

By focusing on the particular ministry that our Meeting has to offer at this time, and letting go of other responsibilities that have become burdens, we might rediscover the vitality of the 'concern-orientated life' described by Thomas Kelly as our lives and our Meetings become simplified by 'faithfulness to a few concerns' (*Quaker faith & practice* 20.36).

The testimony
of a transformed life

One of the most important of the original Quaker insights is that our testimony is what we do. It is not what we say we believe or what we claim to value that matters, but what we say with our life. Our testimony is all of our actions – a whole way of life that testifies to the reality of our experience of God. If we have encountered spiritual reality and been changed by it we will lead a transformed life, and that is our testimony.

The specific actions of Quaker testimony have always been very varied, and have changed over time in response to different situations. For the first Quakers the most important forms of testimony were plain and truthful speech and the refusal to pay church tithes. Later, Quaker testimony developed in many directions, including opposition to slavery and war, support for refugees and prison reform. It is only since the 1950s that all of these very diverse kinds of Quaker testimony have been grouped into the familiar lists, like 'Simplicity, Truth, Equality and Peace', simply as a convenient way of explaining and interpreting them.

Unfortunately, since then we have got into the habit of talking about the Quaker testimonies as though they were a list of principles or values that we are supposed to accept, and then try (and inevitably fail) to 'live up to'. Testimonies have become ideas in our heads that we have to work out how to apply to real life. This emphasis on a list of values tends to undermine what is most essential about the Quaker way; that it is a way of practice, rooted in experience, not in principles or beliefs.

Testimony is our faithfulness to the promptings of love and truth in our hearts. It is what fills the heart and flows into action. Testimony is faithful, Spirit-led action that aims to communicate, to challenge and to transform relationships and power structures.

Our corporate testimony is all of those actions that we have discerned together as a Yearly Meeting, including the rejection of violence and the commitments to peace-making, speaking truthfully, refusing to participate in gambling or speculation and becoming a low-carbon community. These aspects of our life together are not an arbitrary list of rules or principles. Quaker testimony aims to reveal something true about the nature of reality, the world as it really is, not just our personal, subjective values.

By reminding us of the ways in which Friends continue to be led into action, these corporate testimonies can help to sensitise us to areas where the Inward Guide may be nudging us in our own lives. Each of us will be led differently at different times, because we all have our own unique experiences, talents and contribution to offer to the world.

One of the gifts of being in community is that each of us brings something different, and none of us has to try to do everything. We may be led to testify in different ways, but if our leadings are genuine all of our actions will harmonise and complement each other because they all flow from and point towards the same reality. Through the discernment of the whole community we are helped to see where our own blind spots and resistances are, to become more aware of the areas where we are less inclined to heed the promptings of love and truth in our hearts.

The aim is not to be morally perfect, but simply to become more whole, more true to reality and faithful to the way that the Spirit is moving within us, for our own flourishing and for the healing of the world.

Spiritual generosity

For many years, Quakers in Britain have been deeply reluctant to share the riches of the Quaker way with others. We have labelled any attempt to welcome potential new Friends as 'proselytising', but as Paul Parker, recording clerk of Britain Yearly Meeting, has pointed out: 'There is a big difference between proselytising and *not hiding*.' Our long-standing refusal to actively invite newcomers is not just liberal reticence. It is a failure of generosity and of imagination, an inability to imagine that people who are not 'just like us' might also find something of value in Quaker practices.

By refusing to reach out to people beyond our existing social circles, expecting them instead to 'find us when they are ready' without any assistance from us, we have become narrowly self-selecting in our social make-up. The culture of British Quakers is now dominated by the views and experiences of a very restricted social group: largely white, retired and overwhelmingly from the education and health professions. There are many good and valuable things about this subculture, but it is inevitably very limited in its range of experience and perspective on the world.

We have unintentionally backed ourselves into a subcultural ghetto, which both restricts the range of insights available to our ministry and discernment, and also makes it extremely difficult for the vast majority of people in our society not to feel uncomfortably out of place in any of our Meetings.

In recent years, initiatives such as Quaker Quest and national Quaker Week have challenged Friends to overcome this exclusive 'culture of hiddenness'. Meetings which have done this have often encountered unexpected benefits, as Friends have learned much more about each other, quite apart from the energy and enthusiasm brought by new attenders. Even those Meetings which have experimented with some form of outreach, however, are not always clear about the reason for doing it. Is it in order to grow as a Meeting, to prevent Quakers in Britain from dying out, or for some other reason?

The Religious Society of Friends is not an end in itself, but a vehicle for nurturing the spiritual practices that can sustain a more fully human life – one that is guided by and surrendered to the 'principle of life within'. What Quakers in Britain have to share with others is a tradition of spiritual practice that enables us to encounter a source of healing, guidance, meaning and purpose within ourselves, and the quality of the community life that emerges from sharing these practices together. The motivation for our outreach is spiritual generosity towards all of those people who are experiencing the confusion, meaninglessness and disconnection that are so characteristic of our times.

Authentic spiritual practices are remedies for the soul-sickness of a culture that suppresses and distorts our inner lives in order to keep selling us distraction. The Quaker way offers a path through the modern condition of meaninglessness and isolation by drawing us into the purposes of God, by which our own healing and growth into maturity are brought to participate in the healing of the world.

Spiritual generosity challenges all of us to move outside our comfortable social ghettos and to share the life-giving riches of the Quaker way with people of different cultures, experiences and life-journeys. We need to be willing to enlarge our image of what a Quaker community might look, sound and act like. We need the generosity to reach out to welcome those whose differences can enlarge and enrich our experience of Quaker community, and our insights into the leadings of the Spirit for our times.

Other pieces

Quaker renewal

A new Quakerism?

Is a new form of the Quaker Way emerging for the twenty-first century? Throughout our history British Quakers have been able to transform our Society when old forms no longer served as vehicles for the Spirit.

Each period of Quaker history, from eighteenth-century Quietism to nineteenth-century Evangelicalism and twentieth-century Liberalism, began with a creative renewal of spirituality and witness. As each of these forms gradually diminished in relevance and vitality, a new transformation of Quakerism emerged to meet contemporary needs.

Liberal Quakerism has been the dominant form of Quaker spirituality in Britain Yearly Meeting for over a century. Its continuing appeal is eloquently expressed by the Meeting house sign quoted in Gerald Hewitson's Swarthmore Lecture:

> Quakers are people of different beliefs, lifestyles and social backgrounds. What we have in common is an acceptance that all people are on a spiritual journey. We hope that we are indeed a real society of Friends, open to the world and welcoming everyone.

For many Friends today, especially those who have been hurt or excluded by traditional churches, a Quaker Meeting is primarily a 'safe space' – a place to be themselves, where they will be accepted for who they are, without expectations or demands. Among Friends they find a liberating acceptance of differences in lifestyle and sexuality, without any oppressive leaders trying to impose rulings on acceptable belief and behaviour.

However, in recent decades Liberal Quakerism has unmistakeably declined in spiritual coherence and vitality, as well as membership. Although Friends are engaged in a huge range of social action, we no longer have a shared language with which to communicate our spiritual experience, or a shared understanding of core Quaker practices such as Meeting for Worship, testimony or discernment. We have retreated from sharing our spiritual experience with each other and with the wider society. Consequently, we have shrunk to a predominantly white, middle-class group of retired people, while complacently assuring ourselves that 'people will find us when they are ready', without the need for any action on our part.

We have cultivated a marked hostility to spiritual teaching, insisting that 'Quakerism is caught not taught', and as a result many Friends who have been members for decades remain ignorant about traditional Quaker practices and spirituality. We have become intolerant of any suggestion of leadership or authority, and by failing to encourage and support each other's gifts and leadings we have deprived ourselves of direction. We have become collections of like-minded (because socially similar) individuals, rather than true communities of people who are both accountable to and responsible for each other.

We rejected Quaker tradition, with its fervent early Friends and old-fashioned religious language, and ended up with a Quakerism that is almost devoid of religious content, in which our spiritual experience is something private that we cannot share with each other. Consequently, we have little to offer people seeking a deeper spiritual reality, beyond an accepting space for their own solitary spiritual searchings.

The current trajectory of Liberal Quakerism is towards a secular friendly society, which has replaced any spiritual content with a vague concept of Quaker 'values' that are almost indistinguishable from the background liberal middle-class culture. With nothing deeper to offer people who are genuinely seeking a path of spiritual transformation, such a Quakerism would no longer have any distinctive identity or any reason to exist.

However, there are signs of an emerging alternative to the continued dilution of Quakerism in Britain. We cannot anticipate what this new form of Quakerism might eventually look like, but hints are appearing in some of the conversations that are bubbling up across Britain Yearly Meeting.

These characteristics are striking because of some radical departures from Liberal Quaker orthodoxy. They include a number of themes.

First, a desire for deeper, more disciplined worship and spiritual practice. Many Friends seek a more powerful experience of Quaker spirituality. They want to know the transformative power of truly gathered worship at the centre of their lives and communities. Increasingly, Meetings are exploring the Quaker meditation practice of 'Experiment with Light', or experimenting with semi-programmed or extended Meetings for Worship, spiritual friendships, silent retreats, journaling and other spiritual disciplines beyond an hour on Sunday mornings.

Second, recognising the need for leadership that empowers others, and that supports and encourages the development of everyone's ministry. This understanding of leadership includes a renewed attention to the value of eldership, spiritual accompaniment, travelling ministry and spiritual teaching.

Third, a willingness to work towards a shared understanding of the Quaker Way and a new clarity of language to communicate the experience of spiritual reality, God, worship and prayer. As one Friend at a Kindlers conference said: 'At each stage in the Quaker past Friends have been clear about these things; we need to become clear about them too, knowing that our clarity may not be their clarity.' This shared language will not be imposed by any group, but may emerge through a process of 'threshing' throughout Britain Yearly Meeting.

Fourth, deliberately reaching out to the wider society with a confident Quaker message and invitation. Since the spread of Quaker Quest (initially resisted by many Friends as 'proselytising') there has been a growing enthusiasm for Quaker outreach, including initiatives such as Quaker Week. This is often accompanied by a conscious intention to create more diverse Quaker communities – socially, ethnically and generationally.

Fifth, a re-engagement with Quaker tradition. There is a growing interest in the spirituality of early Friends, reflected in recent Swarthmore Lectures and the popularity of Experiment with Light. In the foundational insights of the first period of Quakerism, many Friends are rediscovering the passion and authenticity of Quaker spirituality and looking for ways to live and express it in contemporary forms.

Sixth, a willingness to overhaul Quaker structures and bureaucracy to serve the spiritual practice of the community. Some Meetings, overburdened and exhausted by the pressure to fill nominations for Local, Area and national committees, have laid down all of their roles while they re-examine their real priorities from scratch. A renewed focus on the spiritual priorities of the community seems likely to require a drastic slimming down of Quaker structures. In many communities they are no longer serving the life of the Spirit.

These signs of an emerging 'new Quakerism' suggest that the Quaker movement in Britain may not be condemned to the gradual winding-down that has been predicted by many Friends. Perhaps, once again, the Spirit is acting among us to bring a new, creative and re-energised form of Quakerism into the world. We don't yet know what it will look like. However, if our past experience is any guide, it will draw on the deepest insights of our tradition, but express them in a way that is very different to any form of Quakerism that has gone before.

Friends and family

When I joined Quakers I was drawn to becoming part of an 'extended family' of Quakers past and present. It is a family that contains some wonderful ancestors and fascinating far-flung cousins, as well as its full share of rather peculiar aunts and uncles.

By becoming a Quaker, I felt that I was being accepted into the shared life of this worldwide, centuries-old Quaker family. I was no longer just an individual seeker on a solitary spiritual journey, but part of a people with its own stories and culture, sometimes baffling or infuriating, but now also part of my story too.

Those of us who have grown up in British society have been taught to value above all else the virtues of freedom, privacy, independence and individuality. These are important values, but without a balancing experience of rootedness in a wider community the absence of belonging leaves many of us with a pervasive sense of emptiness and isolation. These are symptoms of the starvation of our soul-needs for connection, identity, meaning, value and purpose.

In more traditional societies, such as Zimbabwe, where I lived with my family at the Hlekweni Friends Training Centre a few years ago, this condition of drastic solitude is very rare. In rural Africa you know who you are through your kinship relations and the shared stories, ancestors and religion of your people – as expressed in the ubiquitous African proverb: 'A person is a person through other people.' Zimbabwean families can, of course, be places of conflict and oppression, particularly for women and young people.

But they also hold their members in a web of relationships and responsibilities that grounds their identity as part of a people.

In Zimbabwe we discovered how Sheffield Friends had become 'our people'. They showed us generous care beyond anything we had anticipated. Even people who knew us slightly wrote letters and sent parcels, and gave money to support us when we needed help.

For me, this experience was a reminder of our participation in what early Friends called 'a gathered people'. A gathered people is not just an association of individuals who happen to share overlapping values or interests. It is formed by the raising and quickening of a new spiritual life and power within each person.

When we recognise the life of the Spirit being kindled in another person, it calls forth an answering response in us; this is what early Friends meant by 'answering that of God' in others. Recognising this same Spirit at work in each other draws us into a bond of mutual belonging, which is lived out through caring, conflict and forgiveness.

This is the experience described by Francis Howgill, the early Quaker, in this famous passage from *Quaker faith & practice* 19.08:

> *And from that day forward, our hearts were knit unto the Lord and one unto another in true and fervent love, in the covenant of Life with God; and that was a strong obligation or bond upon all our spirits, which united us one unto another.*

As modern Quakers, how can we recover this experience of being a gathered people? It means recognising that we are not just isolated individuals on our own spiritual journeys. We are also part of a living community and a current of spiritual awakening that links us to Friends in the past and future throughout the world.

Return within

The goal of the Quaker way is so simple that it can be summed up in one sentence. It is to become completely responsive to the leadings of the Inward Guide. In the beautiful words of Francis Howgill:

> Return, return to Him that is the first Love, and the first-born of every creature, who is the Light of the world... Return home to within, sweep your houses all, the groat is there, the little leaven is there, the grain of mustard-seed you will see, which the Kingdom of God is like... and here you will see your Teacher not removed into a corner, but present when you are upon your beds and about your labour, convincing, instructing, leading, correcting, judging and giving peace to all that love and follow Him.

> *Quaker faith & practice*, 26.71

This is all that is needed for our healing and happiness, for the reconciliation of the world and the flourishing of our relationship with the earth. If each person simply became fully responsive to the 'promptings of love and truth' in their hearts, then war, economic exploitation and environmental destruction would be impossible, and the Beloved Community would flourish. This is what all of our Quaker practices, culture and organisation exist for, and the sole test of their validity is whether they are useful for guiding people into this capacity for spiritual attention and responsiveness to the Inward Light.

This way of attentiveness and faithfulness to the Spirit doesn't depend on any specific beliefs, but it can be inhibited by our own actions, our unconscious resistance, or by any belief system that requires us to ignore crucial aspects of our own experience, or to close our hearts to people defined as 'other'. These can include dogmatic rationalism just as much as some religious or political ideologies.

Unfortunately, by the time that we come to adulthood each of us is already to a greater or lesser extent opposed to the Light within us; somehow we have all armoured ourselves against the in-breaking of the Light.

The religious path is simply the process of dissolving these defences, becoming more aware, sensitive and open to the inner guidance that is always available. To anyone who has seriously tried to follow a religious path it is obvious that this is far easier said than done, but there are many practices that can be helpful in this process. I would like to share some of the practices that have been most important for me, and invite you to reflect on your own.

- Making deliberate choices to protect ourselves from mental pollution, overwork, excessive busyness, noise and constant distraction. Taking time to become aware of our own feelings, thoughts and surroundings, and the needs and feelings of those around us.

- Making a regular discipline of one or more practices that focus our intention and attention. A regular practice such as prayer, meditation, journaling, spiritual reading, mindful movement, and so on, helps to remind us of our intention to return to awareness. Discipline is important, because staying with a practice even when it becomes uncomfortable or boring is often when we discover the aspects of ourselves that we have been hiding from.

- Finding a supportive community and investing in relationships with people who can encourage and challenge us. Friendship is a crucial and often-neglected aspect of the spiritual path, which is too often represented as a solitary, individual task. None of us is strong enough to do it on our own. We need friends around us who can sustain us when we are confused or discouraged, and who are willing to share their questions and struggles.

- Allowing our lives to be shaped by the ethical guidance of a mature tradition, such as the Quaker *Advices & queries*. This can help us to avoid falling into some of the most common traps that tend to deaden our empathy for others. Adopting some ethical guidelines doesn't mean striving to fulfil impossible ideals of perfection. Instead, we could see them as supports for the quality of life and consciousness that helps us to stay awake and attentive to the Spirit.

Above all, perhaps, we need to decide not to despair of ourselves; to accept that we are not perfect and never will be, and to forgive ourselves for our failures and inner resistance. The religious path is not a self-improvement project. We do not need to labour to perfect ourselves, only to return to ourselves, to our capacity to listen and respond to the Inward Guide.

All of us have a tendency to become trapped by our own identity, habits and opinions. Many of us carry a burden of hardened attitudes and accumulated habits that seem to weigh us down; very often it is only the suffering caused by our own failures that finally breaks through our defences, wakes us up and enables us to turn around.

It is the moment when we become conscious of our distance from God, our refusal of the Light; that is the critical opportunity, the blessed season. Perhaps it is only this that will enable us to take our life seriously, to recognise that it is bigger than our own small stories about ourselves, and begin to sense the great mystery of our own life.

Being released from our habit-formed carapace of behaviours, attitudes and obsessions opens up the possibility of spontaneity in how we respond to the world. This quality of spontaneity is often noticeable among people who are on a path of opening to the Spirit. As a fairly new attender at our Meeting once observed, 'the thing about the Quakers I've met is you never know what they are going to say next'.

We also need great patience with ourselves (and others), recognising that the habits of inner resistance are often loosened only with the passage of many years. Luke Cock, the early Friend, could be a model for us of this quality of patience, testifying that:

> *I said to my Guide, 'Nay, I doubt I never can follow up here: but don't leave me: take my pace, I pray Thee, for I mun rest me.' So I tarried here a great while, till my wife cried, 'We'se all be ruined: what is thee ganging stark mad to follow t'silly Quakers?' Here I struggled and cried, and begged of my Guide to stay and take my pace: and presently my wife was convinced. 'Well,' says she, 'now follow thy Guide, let come what will. The Lord hath done abundance for us: we will trust in Him.' Nay, now, I thought, I'll to my Guide again, now go on, I'll follow Thee truly; so I got to the end of this lane cheerfully…*

> *My Guide led me up another lane, more difficult than any of the former, which was to bear testimony to that Hand that had done all this for me. This was a hard one: I thought I must never have seen the end of it. I was eleven years all but one month in it.*

> *Quaker faith & practice*, 20.22

Christian 'roots'

British Quakers often describe our relationship to Christianity with the expression 'Christian roots'. The meaning of this expression is equivocal, because it is an attempt to reconcile Quakerism's origin as a radical Christian movement with some modern Friends' widespread rejection of Christianity. Are our Christian 'roots' what we are anchored in, and continue to draw nourishment from, or what we historically grew from, but have now left behind?

Perhaps the most interesting aspect of these conflicting attitudes is that both those Friends who reject Christianity and those who defend it often share an understanding of Christianity that was explicitly rejected by the first Quakers.

Early Friends described the Quaker movement as 'primitive Christianity revived', but they had a distinctive interpretation of Christianity that was passionately opposed to the orthodox Protestant theology of their day. The first Quakers rejected religious dogmatism, authoritarianism and collusion with powerful elites quite as vehemently as any modern-day nontheist. Early Quakers believed that they had rediscovered the core insights of Jesus and the first Christians, which official Church teachings had systematically evaded, ignored or misrepresented since the first century.

The Quaker understanding of Christianity emphasises the primacy of inward experience of spiritual reality – the 'Inward Christ'. Early Friends understood 'Christ' as an inward reality, accessible to every person by experience, to guide and empower them to live the kind of life that Jesus lived.

Faith in Christ means trusting in this Inward Guide, which enlightens everyone who is willing to open their lives to it. The Inward Christ is luminously present in the life and words of Jesus of Nazareth that are recorded in the Bible, but in a more obscure degree it is present, if only as a potential, in every person – this is what George Fox meant by 'that of God in everyone'.

This understanding of Christian faith is not an intellectual commitment to a set of abstract propositions about the nature of the Trinity and the atonement, or beliefs about the creation of the world or the afterlife. It is a practical commitment to living in a way that is illuminated and guided by the inward spirit of Christ in daily life:

> ...here you will see your Teacher not removed into a corner, but present when you are upon your beds and about your labour, convincing, instructing, leading, correcting, judging and giving peace to all that love and follow Him.

Francis Howgill, *Lamentation for the Scattered Tribes*, 1656

Robert Barclay distinguished between these two ways of knowing:

> ...the saving heart-knowledge, and the soaring, airy head-knowledge. The last, we confess, may be diverse ways obtained; but the first, by no other way than the inward immediate manifestation and revelation of God's Spirit, shining in and upon the heart, enlightening and opening the understanding.

Apology for the True Christian Divinity, 1678

For George Fox and other early Quakers, there was no value in simply holding an opinion about Christ, or in any religious 'notions' whatsoever. All the traditional Christian 'beliefs' – in the incarnation, resurrection, atonement, redemption and so on, are primarily symbolic expressions of experience. They have no meaning as verbal doctrines or intellectual commitments; their only value is as descriptions of real states of awareness and relationship. The 'soaring, airy head-knowledge' cannot help us. Real Christian faith is knowing the power of the inward presence of Christ, experiencing its struggle with the darkness of addiction and temptation within us, and coming to live a transformed life of selflessness and integrity.

This was the transformative experience Friends called 'convincement', and in it they recognised all the symbolic imagery of the Bible, come alive as vivid depictions of their own reality. For Quakers the Bible was never the primary source of religious revelation and authority but, as a record of the discernment and actions of others who have been led by the Spirit, it is useful for testing our own often uncertain discernment. George Fox claimed that everything he had discovered 'experimentally' through the direct openings of the Spirit he later found confirmed in the Bible, but also that even 'if there was no scripture… Christ [that is, the inward spirit of Christ] is sufficient' (Epistle 320, 1676).

Early Friends believed that as people come to follow the leadings of the Spirit of Christ, we begin to share in the life of communion with God and with each other that Jesus called 'the Kingdom of God'. According to Jesus, the Kingdom of God is a new social reality that favours the poor and excluded. The core of Jesus' teaching was this 'good news to the poor' that the reign of God is on its way, growing invisibly throughout humanity like yeast through dough – 'the Kingdom of God is among you' (Luke 17:21). This Kingdom of God will be fulfilled through the lives of ordinary and disregarded people, as they are transformed by the Spirit of Christ within; turning away from the seductions of power, wealth and status, to embrace a life based on sharing and reconciliation.

Many contemporary Christian Friends have come to Quakers from mainstream churches and their understanding of Christianity is often recognisably Anglican, Methodist or Catholic, rather than Quaker. Similarly, Friends who are hostile to Christianity are often reacting against their experience of mainstream church teachings and institutions, rather than the Quaker understanding of what it means to be a Christian – a follower of the inward spirit of Christ that is continually speaking within every person.

Light, Seed and Guide

When Quakers talk about spiritual reality they often produce lists of substitute words, such as 'God, the Divine, the Tao, Goddess, or whatever you call it'. The implication seems to be that all of these terms are synonymous, and the point of the list is to indicate that diverse names and beliefs are equally acceptable, and are all talking about the same thing. The specific connotations of different words are usually downplayed, because the list is a way of signalling our openness to theological diversity, rather than describing our own spiritual experience.

By contrast, the religious language of early Quakers was not concerned with abstract theological gestures, but with communicating real personal experience. Early Friends avoided the tendency of much mainstream Christian theology to try to tie down spiritual reality into neat categories that can be intellectually mastered, independently of our own lived experience. The first generation of Quakers created a shared vocabulary that was extraordinarily rich in symbolism and metaphor, rather than a system of precise theological definitions.

Early Friends used a great diversity of spiritual language, drawing on the rich metaphorical resources of the Bible as well as inventing their own terms, such as 'the Inward Light', 'the Seed', 'the Principle of Life', 'the Guide', 'the Inward Teacher', 'Inward Christ' and many others. This rich vocabulary was not just a list of interchangeable synonyms. The different metaphors expressed the diverse range of personal spiritual experience, and hinted at the multifaceted nature of ultimate reality.

The language used by modern Quakers draws on a much wider range of religious traditions, but our specifically Quaker vocabulary is rather thin by comparison. The most popular modern Quaker religious metaphor is probably that of 'the Inner Light'. The symbolism of light suggests something that reveals and informs. This is, of course, an important aspect of Quaker spirituality, but it is far from the whole of it.

Douglas Gwyn has contrasted this modern focus on the metaphor of light with the more neglected early Quaker language of the 'seed':

> We speak of the light to describe the revealing, guiding, discerning aspects of God's presence within. By contrast, the language of the seed hints at other aspects, ones we are more likely to avoid. Early Friends wrote of the seed as the **power** of God, the **promise** of God, the **inheritance** of God sown within each human heart. It is sown there in compassion toward us, sown in the hope that each one of us will become a true and faithful child of God. But this seed within germinates and rises to new life only as we sink down to it.

> The Seed is the power of God's will. While the light reveals God's will to us, lets us **know** it, the seed is about the **power to do it here and now**. Or again, while the light inspires in us thoughts that are not necessarily our thoughts, the seed raises a will in us that is not necessarily our will. That implies that there is some kind of **death** to be encountered in ourselves if we are to know the power of the seed.

> Sink Down to the Seed, 1996

There are, of course, many other aspects of spiritual experience that call for attentive naming. Another key early Quaker metaphor was that of the 'Inward Guide'. The image of the guide perhaps points us towards an area of experience that links the seed and the light. The guide *draws us towards* what the light *reveals*. It creates the willingness to 'sink down to the Seed', to give our consent to the new will that is gradually germinating within us.

I understand this guide not just in the sense of one who shows the way, but also as the one who reveals to us the beauty of the journey, and awakens a desire to follow. It is the voice of the guide that is heard by the prophet Hosea in the Bible: 'So then, I Myself will entice her, I will bring her into the wilderness and speak to her heart.' Hosea (2:14)

The Inward Guide could stand for that aspect of our inner experience that awakens to the beauty of life when it is lived from the seed of God within.

Often, the Guide speaks to us through the example of others' lives, revealing the attractiveness of compassion, generosity and courage, and awakening a desire to discover our own potential for these qualities. We have encountered the Guide at those times when the world appears illuminated by the possibility of selflessness and communion; when we sense the promise that 'the world will be saved by beauty' (Fyodor Dostoevsky, *The Idiot*, 1868).

True inward transformation is not effected purely by ethical idealism or a sense of duty. It relies on longing desire; a movement of the heart that opens us to the possibilities of a richer, more beautiful and selfless life.

People whose hearts are awakened in this way become willing to surrender themselves, to sink down to the seed, to consent to become someone else for other people. Simplifying their lives, sharing their possessions, and even physical risk and hardship become easy and attractive in the course of this movement. They willingly and enthusiastically abandon anything that hinders them from pursuing the 'pearl of great price', the new richness of life that has been revealed to them.

Quaker renewal

Signs of hope

Whell our daughter Moya was born we held a 'welcoming' celebration for her at home, reading out this passage from the prophet Isaiah:

See, I am doing a new thing! Now it springs up; do you not perceive it? I am making a way in the wilderness and streams in the wasteland.

Isaiah 43:19

For us, the birth of our first child was a sign of hope for the future, simply because her life was 'a new thing' – filled with utterly unpredictable potential for bringing beauty and joy and healing into the world.

Hope is not the same as optimism. It does not mean believing that things will inevitably improve or anticipating the sudden disappearance of all our problems. Hope is also possible alongside a clear perception of the consequences of our own destructiveness and the persistence of violence and injustice. But an attitude of hope means an openness to the future, recognising that the future is not fixed in a mechanical, unrelenting pattern, because it will result from the actions of innumerable people, all of whom are capable of unpredictable acts of creativity and generosity.

The Quaker movement was formed in a period when many people's expectations of the future had been crushed by political events. Many early Friends had been deeply committed to the parliamentary cause during the English civil war. They lived through the failure of the Commonwealth government,

Oliver Cromwell's dictatorship and, finally, the restoration of the monarchy. Friends did not respond to the failure of their hopes and the reimposition of political and religious absolutism by armed resistance, nor did they simply submit to the new restrictions on religious freedom. Instead, almost uniquely among the nonconformist sects of the time, they sustained a persistent, public commitment to living the Truth they had encountered, despite systematic and intense state persecution.

Quakers, at this time, emphasised the power of 'testimony' – of living a life of utter integrity and faithfulness to God's purposes – challenging and transforming situations of untruth and injustice. They experienced the reality that living an authentic human life, and maintaining a genuine human community, is a political act. Rex Ambler has described it as 'lives lived in the truth'.

This kind of influence may seem inadequate to the huge and urgent political challenges of our time. The influence of individuals and small groups on those around them is unlikely to save us from the long-term economic and ecological crises that we are preparing for future generations and ourselves. But however difficult the times our children will live through there will be some people who practise sharing and reconciliation, and some places where a more fully human life and community can flourish, because of the actions of people living now.

This means that how we choose to live matters. It will shape the future for good or ill and affect the lives of people we may never meet or know about. It means trusting in our own capacity for new beginnings, that we are not trapped by our past or confined by our habits and compulsions, and that something new can happen in our own lives.

Rather than despairing or giving way to fatalism, can we be ready to recognise and encourage these signs of hope within and around us, to perceive the times and places where the Spirit is acting to 'do a new thing'?

What is Quakerism for?

One of the ways that early Friends differed most from modern Quakers is that they were able to say with great clarity and conviction just what the purpose of the Quaker Way is:

> The main thing in religion is to keep the conscience pure to the Lord, to know the guide, to follow the guide, to receive from him the light whereby I am to walk; and not to take things for truths because others see them to be truths; but to wait till the spirit makes them manifest to me.

Isaac Penington

In other words, the Quaker Way is a vehicle, a means to direct us towards the Inward Guide, so that we can be taught and guided by the Light in our own consciences. Early Quakers recognised that there is one Inward Teacher, Guide or Spirit, that speaks to all people in all times and places, no matter what their culture or religion. The purpose of Quaker worship, testimony, culture and organisation is nothing else than this – to help us to attend to that Inward Guide and follow it. It is that simple – simple but not easy.

The difficulty that all of us experience in staying close to the guide is the main reason we need to be part of a community. A Quaker community should practise the communal discernment that helps us to distinguish the voice of the Spirit from our own wishes or obsessions. It also preserves the memory of ways that Friends have been led by the Spirit in other times and situations, which can help to sensitise us to how the same Spirit is speaking to us now.

This is also the function of Quaker testimonies. As records of the faithful discernment and action of Friends throughout history, they serve to remind us of the directions in which the Spirit has led Friends in the past, so that we can become more attentive to the 'promptings of love and truth' in our own hearts.

The early Quaker testimonies included a fairly diverse range of specific behaviour including 'plain speech', refusing to fight or swear oaths, and abstaining from gambling and 'frivolous amusements'. These actions arose from specific challenges facing Quaker communities, and their discernment of the ways that the Inward Light was calling them to respond.

The testimonies have changed over time, reflecting changes in society and in Friends' discernment, so that some testimonies have been abandoned or modified (such as plain speech and rejection of music and the arts), while others have emerged or gained in importance, such as the recent recognition of same sex marriage and the Canterbury Commitment.

In recent decades these testimonies have increasingly been translated into a set of abstract principles, usually summarised as 'Simplicity, Truth, Equality and Peace'. The attempt to live perfectly ethical lifestyles by 'applying' Quaker values and principles to our decisions mistakes the signposts for the destination. It frequently leads to a stifling sense of guilt or, worse, self-righteousness as we compare ourselves with others, instead of focussing on the guidance of the Spirit that is particularly for us, at this moment.

Each one of us has a unique calling: we have been given a life that contains unique gifts and a unique opportunity to bring more of God's love, justice and beauty into the world. Our task is to find that calling and to follow it. We won't find our calling by choosing a set of abstract principles of moral perfection and trying to live up to them. The only way is by paying attention to the Inward Guide, and allowing it to lead us into the life that is waiting for us, on a path that nourishes our souls.